$4.00 THE YEAR

ART AND ARCHAEOLOGY

An Illustrated Monthly Magazine

PUBLISHED AT WASHINGTON, D. C., BY

THE ARCHAEOLOGICAL INSTITUTE OF AMERICA

(TITLE REGISTERED U. S. PATENT OFFICE)

VOLUME IX   APRIL, 1920   No. 4

CONTENTS

HELLENISTIC CITIES OF ASIA MINOR

TERMS: $4.00 a year in advance; single numbers, 35 cents. Instructions for renewal, discontinuance, or change of address should be sent two weeks before the date they are to go into effect.

All correspondence should be addressed and remittances made to ART & ARCHAEOLOGY, the Octagon, Washington, D. C. Also manuscripts, photographs, material for notes and news, books for review, and exchanges, should be sent to this address.

Advertisements should be sent to CHANDLER & Co., Advertising Managers, 1 West 34th St., New York, N. Y.

A detail from the altar of Zeus, at Pergamum, Athena fighting with a giant, Victory flying to crown her, while the goddess Earth rises from the ground to aid her children.

ART and ARCHAEOLOGY

The Arts Throughout the Ages

VOLUME IX   APRIL, 1920   NUMBER 4

HELLENISTIC CITIES OF ASIA MINOR

PREFACE

ASIA MINOR is a name so loosely applied, and one so broad and inclusive, that it requires definition or delimitation, especially when used in connection with so small a collection of brief and summary articles as are included in this number of ART AND ARCHAEOLOGY. These articles are limited, for the most part, to a single period of the art history of Asia Minor, the Hellenistic Period—and, even within this limitation, they are unable to present more than a series of general sketches of the more recent, and more important, archaeological discoveries. It would be a pity if these sketches should convey to the mind of the general reader, who is perhaps unacquainted with the history of Asia Minor, the notion that the Greek and Hellenistic periods are either the only ones worthy of consideration or the only periods which have been the subject of extensive archaeological research. The vast treasure of archaeological material and the wealth of monuments of art, which Asia Minor holds stored among its ruins and hidden beneath its soil, have only begun to be brought to light by the explorers and excavators of the past century. It is important, at this particular time, that the American people should be fully aware of the great importance of this field, when the immediate future of Asia Minor may depend largely upon their will in connection with the League of Nations.

To recall what archaeological material this vast country has buried, hidden, and stored away within its boundaries, a brief survey of its history will prove the best reminder. Lying north and northwest of the Taurus Mountains, Asia Minor reaches out, as an arm of the continent of Asia, between the Mediterranean and the Black Sea, almost to the point of touching Europe at the Dardanelles. "Planted like a bridge between Asia and Europe," it has been, since remote times, the battle-ground of two continents. Its history has been a kaleidoscopic picture of races, ever emigrating westward from the heart of Asia, who have sought to establish states and empires within its area. The history of this ceaseless struggle divides itself into seven broad periods, each period having a more or less distinct artistic and racial character.

[155]

ART AND ARCHAEOLOGY

In the beginning, Asia Minor was inhabited by peoples perhaps not Aryan, of whom the Hittites, who appear in historical records before the year 2000 B.C. were the most aggressive and highly organized. The remains of this civilization, which are scattered over the whole central portion of the peninsula, have only recently begun to attract the interest of the archaeological world through the discoveries at Boghaz Köi. Following the Hittite and non-Aryan period came the Aryan period when new races from the east invaded the country and by the eleventh century before Christ had already commenced to establish separate states. This second period includes the Homeric Age, with its remains at Troy which Schliemann brought to light; it covers the time when Greek colonies settled on the islands and the coast and when Ionian art was in the process of development; and it closes with the overthrow of the Lydians, under the wealthy King Croesus, by the Persians.

The third period, commencing with the conquest of Lydia by the Persian Cyrus in the middle of the sixth century, was short, for the Persian rule was lax and quickly succumbed before the armies of Alexander the Great in the fourth century B.C. Under the Macedonian chieftain and his generals, who divided the land into separate states on Alexander's death, the fourth period was the most productive artistically, for Asia Minor was inoculated with the spirit of Greek culture. This Hellenistic period, with some of whose archaeological remains the papers in this number deal, gave way to the Roman political rule in the second century B.C., without any basic change in the artistic traditions of the country. The Roman period, which is the fifth, extended to the establishment of the Byzantine Empire and the general spread of Christianity throughout Asia Minor in the fourth century A. D.

During the whole of the Roman and Byzantine periods the racial, and hence the artistic, character of the country was undergoing change and modification due to the constant inpouring of Teutonic and Slavic tribes from the north and east. The sixth, or Byzantine period, offers as great archæological material and interest as any of the former periods, for it is coming to be realized that, in all likelihood, the style in art, which we call Byzantine, germinated in, and spread from, Asia Minor.

The Byzantine domination was shaken by the inroads of the Sassanian Persians in the seventh century A.D. These inroads were quickly followed by the Arab conquests and, while the government at Constantinople was able to expel the invaders, the country had once more been subjected to a new racial influence from the Orient. The period, however, extended until the eleventh century when the Seljuk Turks established a grasp on the region which, at a later period, was transferred to the Ottoman Turks whose domination has only recently been shaken and is probably never to be entirely loosened. While the Ottoman rule has been productive of little which is of artistic value and has been responsible for the cloud of ignorance and mystery which has lain over the historical and archæological remains of Asia Minor, the Seljuk Turk was a lover and producer of art in his own way. The remains of his artistic activity which are still to be seen in his mosques and palaces are scarcely less interesting and valuable than those of former periods.

Now that the history of Asia Minor stands on the threshold of a new era, the archaeological world can only hope that the eighth period, be it American, British, Greek, or Allied, will provide a government which will open this store-house to the world and preserve its treasures for future generations.

EDITOR.

[156]

Figure 2.—Restoration of the Acropolis of Pergamum. (*After Thiersch and Blaum.*)

PERGAMUM AND EPHESUS

By David M. Robinson

THE remains of the crowned spots are indeed of surpassing interest and importance. Earth proudly wears the Parthenon as the best gem upon her zone, that most splendid jewel which shines on the Athenian acropolis, but it is impossible rightly to understand the history of ancient Greece or of Athens itself without some knowledge of the Holy Land of Asia Minor, that immense land of beautiful landscapes and flowing rivers, the America of antiquity, which forms such a splendid natural contrast to barren Attica, and which was indeed the greatest secret of the power of the Greeks in earlier as well as in Hellenistic times. There is not space for me to discuss the whole of Asia Minor, and as the other articles in this number of ART AND ARCHAEOLOGY deal with several of the Greek and Roman sites, I have been asked to limit myself to two of the seven branches of the Asia Minor candlestick, Pergamum and

Ephesus. Even with this limitation it will be possible in the space allotted to me only to give a sketch of the two ancient cities in the Near East which were so important in Hellenistic and Roman times.

Pergamum (Fig. 1), one of the seven Biblical churches, the city which invented parchment when the jealous Egyptian kings cut off the supply of paper or papyrus and gave its name Pergamena to the new invention, was perhaps the most celebrated town of Asia Minor. It was, however, only a small settlement till the beginning of the third century B. C. when, according to Strabo, the Augustan geographer, Lysimachus deposited there in the care of Philetaerus his treasury of 9,000 talents or about nine million dollars. After the death of Lysimachus, Philetaerus, in a somewhat modern spirit, appropriated the treasure, and made himself king of Pergamum from 283 to 263 B. C. In 281 he joined Seleucus

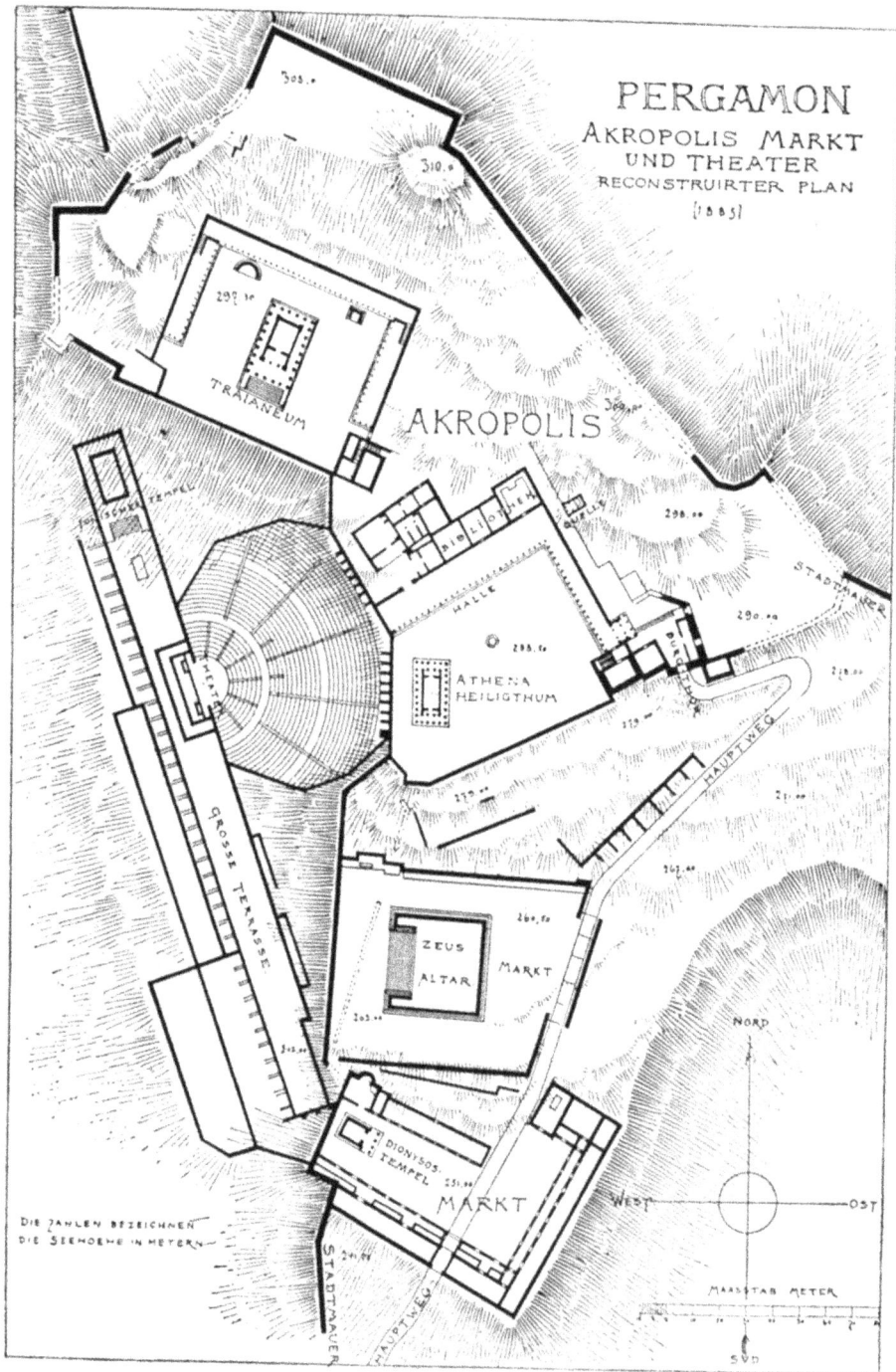

Figure 1.—Plan of the Acropolis of Pergamum. (*From Fabricius.*)

Figure 3.—The Acropolis of Pergamum. (*Photograph of D. M. Robinson.*)

and married his brother Attalus to a Seleucid princess Antiochis and founded the city of Philetaireia. The son of his brother Eumenes (263–241) and his own son Attalus overcame the Syrians and Gauls and brought the kingdom of Pergamum to its height. Under Eumenes II, who ruled from 197 to 159 B. C., and under his successors Attalus II and III, many important buildings were erected, and art found such a foothold that a Pergamene school of literature and art arose. The Pergamenian kings became the Medici of antiquity. Here still remain the foundations of the library, which contained two hundred thousand rolls or volumes, given by Antony to Cleopatra (according to Plutarch) and later transferred to Alexandria, and I suppose it became a part of that great collection, part of which Julius Caesar destroyed, the rest of which Amr, the Arab general of Omar is said—perhaps wrongly—to have destroyed in 640 A. D. because "If these writings of the Greeks agree with the books of God, they are useless and need not be preserved; if they disagree, they are pernicious and ought to be destroyed." Here the wonderful reliefs (frontispiece) representing the fight of the gods with the giants which adorned the altar of Zeus (Fig. 2), or seat of Satan, as it is called in the book of Revelation, built perhaps by Attalus II, and not Eumenes II, were discovered some time since and taken to Berlin. There in the Pergamum Museum the altar was reconstructed. But it was since discovered from a Pergamene coin that the reconstruction was faulty. The old museum was pulled down, and an entirely new one is being erected for a new reconstruction. Shut up in the Berlin Museum the reliefs seem overpowering and oppressive, but if one thinks of them on the altar, high up on the hill of Pergamum, and visible from afar, they become great works of technical art and skill. One of the illustrations shows the ancient acropolis (Fig. 3), a rock rising 270 metres above the plain, self-centred in impregnable strength. To the west the Selinus stream divides the Turkish quarter of modern Bergama on its right bank from the Greek quarter on the left bank. The Cetius flows some distance to the east, and both empty into the Caicus about two miles away. Bergama is a thriving modern village, but owing to the bad roads which connect it with the sea at Dikeli and with the

[159]

Figure 4.—The House of the Consul Attalus. (*From Athenische Mitteilungen, xxxii, 1907, pl. xv.*)

French railway at Soma—a rough drive of about six hours in either case, as I can testify from two visits—its trade in wine, olives, cotton and silk is mostly local. Above the town where there are remains of Roman baths, a theatre, and amphitheatre with a stream flowing through its middle, and other ruins, you can see the ancient road ascending the steep slopes to the plateau, which inclines toward the south.

On this long road with its pavement well-preserved in long stretches, there are several important ancient things to see to-day which the Germans under Conze and Dörpfeld have excavated. We can only briefly enumerate some of them. There is an important south gate with an interesting system of towers and gateways, through which the road passes. There is a lower market place (the upper one being near the altar of Zeus) where time was told by a peculiar clock consisting of a Hermes with a cornucopia out of which water flowed at definite intervals. The market police had their offices here and business was conducted in two-story porticoes which surrounded on all sides an open court, paved with trachyte, 34 by 64 m., where later a Christian church was built. The forty-four or more shops were let out to private persons and in at least one case the rent was paid to one of the temples. The life of the market with its merchants and fishermen and other dealers is pictured in inscriptions as noisy and gay and undoubtedly in the bargaining and other features we have the ancestor of the modern bazaars of Constantinople and Smyrna. In the market place were the tables of the money-changers and small change was a

Figure 5.—The middle terrace of the gymnasium. (*Photograph of D. M. Robinson.*)

Figure 6.—The Temple of Hera. (*From Athenische Mitteilungen, xxxvii, 1912, pl. xxxii a.*)

monopoly of the state as to-day in Turkey where one must carry a bag of piasters to avoid loss caused by changing money. We hear of dishonesty and extortion and even "hush money" and Hadrian enacted laws against the bankers and set them up in the agora, fixing the agio and formulating other regulations. The ancient life of Pergamum as we can reconstruct it from inscriptions seems very modern to one who has paid a high rate of exchange for a bridge-ticket at the Galata bridge at Stamboul or has been offered false coins to-day, since the Pergamene money-changers bought up false or old coins and sold them to others. One can see also in ascending the road to the top of the acropolis an old patrician Pergamene house built in the time of the Pergamene kings but much rebuilt in the second century A. D., by the

Roman consul Attalus (Fig. 4). Here was found the Herm and Hermes of Alcamenes, which changed our ideas about the rival of Phidias and the date of his work, a copy of a statue which originally stood in the Propylaea at Athens. Here also were found remarkable mosaics and wall-paintings with interesting scenes.

Excavations have also been completed in the great gymnasium which was built on three terraces. It was erected originally in the second century B. C. in three sections above the long ascending road. But since that time there has been considerable destruction and restoration. It shows the ingenuity of the Greeks in making use of the steep slope of the hill. The lowest terrace is twelve meters below the second, and the second is twelve meters below the third. On the ter-

[162]

Figure 7.—The Theatre at Pergamum. (*Photograph of D. M. Robinson.*)

races were three separate gymnasiums, dedicated respectively to the boys, the ephebes of eighteen to twenty years of age, and the young men. Near a fountain-house on the road there ascends from the lower gymnasium a vaulted stairway to the middle gymnasium. The middle terrace is 150 by 36 meters, and contains at its eastern end a small Corinthian temple (Fig. 5). The northern side is formed by a long double colonnade, which was single in its original form. Above the middle terrace was a cryptoporticus or covered running track which was destroyed by the extension of the upper terrace to the south. The upper terrace is the largest and contained the Panegyric gymnasium where were the public competitions. There is an open court 36 by 74 meters, originally surrounded by a Doric colonnade, which was changed to Corinthian in the time of Hadrian. Numerous rooms opened on to the colonnade, including an Imperial Hall, and a theatre. In the last cam-

paigns of the Germans a precinct of Hera was found on a terrace above the gymnasium, and completely excavated. The fine cult statue of Zeus stood intact, except for the head, on a base in the middle recess of the cella of the temple, with a female statue on either side. Except for the front portico, which was of marble, the trachyte temple, with its mosaic floor, is well preserved (Fig. 6). The temple was erected by Attalus the second (159 B. C.) as an inscription on the architrave shows, and is the earliest marble building at Pergamum; some scholars even think that the statue which was found there is a portrait-statue of him, and not Zeus. To the east of the temple was a stoa, where a fine female portrait-head of the first century B. C. was found. It is part of a statue and wore a golden wreath, as the holes in the hair show.

The narrow terrace which leads to the Ionic temple past the theatre cut in the side of the hill is shown in one of the illustrations (Fig. 7). An inter-

[163]

Figure 8.—Entrance to precinct of Demeter. (*Photograph of D. M. Robinson.*)

esting thing about this theatre is that it had a movable wooden stage-building in Hellenistic times, and down to Roman times. The sockets into which it could be set are still visible. When no performance was on, the stage was removed, so that people could pass by to the temple of Dionysus. Near this terrace is another, which proved recently to be a precinct of Demeter and her daughter Persephone. In the foreground are the ruins of a temple and altar, to the right the underground rooms of a portico which was 91½ metres long, with three rows of columns and commanded a beautiful view over the valley of the Caicus. In the distance are two columns of a gateway or Propylon, which have been re-erected (Fig. 8). This temple was originally dedicated about 262 B. C. to Demeter alone, but a portico of six columns was added to the temple by the Roman G. Claudius Seilianus Aesimus, in whose behalf an altar was erected near the gateway or Propylon to virtue and temperance by Julia Pia, his wife.

The dedication was made to include Kore also, as the inscription on the later architrave informs us (Fig. 9). On the altar, eight metres long, was the inscription: "Eumenes in behalf of his mother Boa to Demeter," which proves that the altar was built at the same time with the temple on the original architrave of which occurs the same inscription. This Eumenes is Eumenes the elder, and not the son of Apollonis, whose name occurs on the Propylon. In front of the Propylon were also found two altars, the one to the left with an inscription to Virtue and Temperance; that to the right with the inscription to Faith and Concord. The unfluted columns with reeds carved on the capitals have been re-erected. To the right is the Roman nymphaeum or reservoir, which has been excavated; and above a sort of Odeum. Here the people could sit and watch the initiations and mysteries and rites in honor of Demeter as at Oropus and Eleusis. Many inscriptions, including perhaps the first epigraphic evidence for a cult

[164]

Figure 9.—Architrave with inscription from precinct of Demeter. (*Photograph of D. M. Robinson.*)

of the unknown god such as St. Paul mentions at Athens, were discovered in the precinct. In a cistern were found several beautiful Roman heads, among them splendid portraits of Augustus and Tiberius. These are now in Constantinople, but at Pergamum one still sees a relief of the three-headed Cerberus, Hades' watch-dog, the hound of hell, who would appropriately find a place in a sanctuary of Demeter and Persephone. Also appropriate is a relief representing the priestess or goddess herself near an altar with torch in one hand and bowl in other. Near her is a steer with its feet on bases, and tied with a rope to a ring in the pavement such as have recently been found at Ephesus and Sardis. There is a similar relief in Athens, and Pausanias mentions a similar group in the Eleusinium at Athens, but the interpretation is doubtful.

The reconstruction of the acropolis (Fig. 1) shows at the top to the left the temple of Trajan, with a colonnade on three sides. Below, on the next lower terrace is the temple of Athena, built in the 4th century, and the two-story colonnade above contained in the rear the library built by Eumenes the second, who is thought by some to have erected the great altar on the next lower terrace about 175 B. C.

EPHESUS.

Ephesus, the church of Waning Enthusiasm, which is forty-eight miles south of Smyrna by rail, is about the only ancient site in Asia Minor which can be easily and comfortably visited. It was one of the twelve Ionian cities, but differed from some of the others in not having a natural and well protected harbor. Beautifully situated on two rocky hills, Mt. Pion and Mt. Coressus, Ephesus had, however, an artificial inner basin which communicated by means of a canal with the River Cayster and so with the sea. Ephesus was inhabited from very early times. After the Phoenicians and Carians came the Ionian Greeks, who entered into friendly relations with the natives and established the cult of the great goddess Diana, whom Asia and all the world

[165]

Figure 10.—Site of the great temple of Diana at Ephesus. (*Photograph of D. M. Robinson.*)

worshipped. Under the Ionians Ephesus flourished, but it was hard pressed by the rising Lydian kingdom, and finally was conquered by Croesus, whose name appears on some column fragments of the great temple of Diana, which have been taken to the British Museum. After the fall of the Lydian kingdom in 546 B. C., Ephesus passed into the hands of the Persians, and remained there until Alexander the Great came in 334. About 290 B.C. Lysimachus changed the site of the city to Mt. Pion, where the Austrians, under the late Benndorf and Heberdey, conducted the excavations. Ephesus shared the fate of other Asia Minor cities in passing under the yoke of Rome but being the terminal of the great commercial route from the interior, it anciently was always a thriving town; and hence perhaps the most important of the seven churches, where St. Paul spent almost three years. He was probably imprisoned here, although what the guides point out as St. Paul's prison was only an old Roman tower in the wall of Lysimachus. Ephesus suffered much from the Goths in 262 A. D., but most of all from the destruction in

the 13th century by the Turks. The ancient harbor has been silted up, making Ephesus an inland city, changing its site according to Biblical prophecy. Such in brief is the history of this important ancient city.

Hogarth's recent excavations at the Artemisium (Fig. 10), which was one of the seven wonders of the world, his unearthing of three earlier temples, and his finding of a wonderful deposit, dating from the time of Solomon, of ivories, gold statuettes, ornaments and coins have been the subject of lectures and a book by Hogarth himself, and of an illustrated article in ART AND ARCHAEOLOGY, v. 1917, pp. 13–19; hence I pass them by and limit myself to the recent Austrian excavations.

The illustration in Fig. 11, shows the theatre where the events recorded in *Acts XIX* took place during the tumult caused by Demetrius the silversmith, who objected to Paul's preaching because its spirituality lessened the sale of the pretty little shrines of Diana; "And the whole city was filled with confusion, and having caught Gaius and Aristarchus, men of Macedonia, Paul's companions, they rushed with

[166]

Figure 11.—The theatre at Ephesus referred to in Acts XIX. (*Photograph of D. M. Robinson.*)

one accord into this building, crying 'great is Diana of the Ephesians'." The theatre is one of the largest in Asia. In the three divisions taken together it had sixty-six rows of seats, and could seat twenty-five to thirty thousand people (Fig. 12). The seats were of common stone veneered, as it were, with marble. The two ends were built up of stupendous masonry, thirty meters high, with arched entrances to the two horizontal passage-ways. Behind the orchestra was the stage. This was six meters wide and nearly three meters high, and was supported by a triple row of columns. It was approached from the sides by two sloping ramps, and from the inside by three staircases. Behind the stage are the remains of a two-story building, with broad passage-ways and rooms which formed the dressing apartments for the actors. The original theatre was built by Lysimachus, but it was much restored in later times, and it is the theatre of the third century A. D. which appears here. The theatre has been a useful quarry for the natives of Ajas-

soluk, and even in the ancient day many stones were taken to build the so-called Gate of Persecution. It formed the entrance to the citadel in Justinian's time, and above the arch were formerly reliefs, one of which represented the death of Patroclus and Hector, whence the gate got its name. From the theatre a large paved street led south towards the Magnesian gate, passing the market place on the right. In the distance to the right are the ruins of the double church of St. Mary Theotokos, one of the oldest Christian churches, which has been entirely excavated during the last few years (Fig. 13). In the southwest corner of the agora has been discovered a circular Greek building about eight meters in diameter, with three courses of well cut stones preserved. The Austrians in general have not dug deep enough to strike Greek things, but this is an exception. Near the round building where the street turns toward the Magnesian gate is the most important building excavated, namely a library built about 115 A. D., at his own

[167]

Figure 12.—The stage of the theatre at Ephesus. (*Photograph of D. M. Robinson.*)

Figure 14.—Ruins of the Library of Celsus at Ephesus. (*Photograph of D. M. Robinson.*)

Figure 13.—Part of Church of St. Mary Theotokos at Ephesus.

Figure 15.—Restoration of the interior of the Library of Celsus. (*After Niemann.*)

expense in honor of his father, Tiberius Julius Celsus Polemaeanus by Tiberius Julius Aquila, who gave many books, and 25,000 denarii for the purchase of other books (Fig. 14). Nine steps, 18 meters broad, flanked by two large bases on which stood statues of Celsus, lead up to the portico of eight columns arranged in pairs. Seven of the column bases still remain in situ. Behind these was a wall broken by three door-ways, whose richly ornamented pilasters, corresponding to the eight columns, still remain in their lower part. Between the pilasters were niches in which stood four statues discovered in fragments by the excavators, representing in human form respectively The Wisdom of Celsus, The Knowledge of Celsus,

The Virtue of Celsus and The Goodwill of Celsus, and a headless statue of Celsus himself has been found. The main library room, entered by three doors, was sixteen and a third meters wide by eleven meters deep. Opposite the middle door at the rear was an apse, (Fig. 15), four and a half meters broad, in which stood an image of Athena, as in the library at Pergamum. In an underground room directly below was the burial place of Celsus, where his sarcophagus has been found. In the walls themselves, in front of which were six columns on the sides and eight at the rear, were rectangular niches half a meter deep, and about three meters high and one meter wide. There were three on the two sides and two on either side of the apse. In these niches, of which there were three stories, wooden shelves were placed for the ancient book-rolls. There was space for about 100,000 books, only half as many as at Pergamum. So many architectural fragments have been discovered that it has been possible to make an accurate reconstruction.

Johns Hopkins University.

[170]

Figure 1.—Ferry across the Maeander at Miletus.

MILETUS, PRIENE AND SARDIS

By HOWARD CROSBY BUTLER

DEVOTEES of ancient Greek culture, even many enthusiastic students of the literature and art of the Classic period of Greece, often forget how much Hellas, or European Greece, owed to Ionia, the Asiatic cradle of Greek civilization. We think of Athens and Sparta, of Corinth and Argos, of Delphi and Olympia, as the most important sites for the study of Greek antiquity; often ignoring the fact that Miletus and Ephesus, Pergamum and Magnesia, Didyma and Colophon, were not only just as important in the history of Greek culture as the cities of Hellas but were perhaps the leaders and teachers of European Greece. We all remember Troy, and, sometimes no doubt, think of the Trojan war as representing eternal enmity between the opposite shores of the Aegean sea, not realizing perhaps that the war made so vivid by Homer was in reality only a family quarrel, and that both sides of the sea were occupied by a single race. A brilliant English archaeologist has said "the Greeks of Western Asia Minor produced the first full bloom of what we call pure Hellenism." One has only to consult his classical dictionary to learn that many of the greatest figures in the art and literature of the Greeks were natives of Asia Minor; and a casual student of the history of free social institutions will discover

[171]

Figure 2.—Retaining wall of the Theatre, at right facing the Cavea.

that Ionia was the land in which the democratic city state first reached full development.

That bold, irregular strip of shore extending from a little above Smyrna southward along the eastern side of the Aegean sea almost to the southeast tip of Asia Minor, which we call the Ionian coast, with its high rocky promontories stretching out to the islands, its deep bays and estuaries into which several great rivers pour a continual deposit of rich soil snatched from the inland mountains, is almost all there ever was of ancient Ionia. In a straight line it measures hardly 60 miles; but the actual coast line would measure fully three times that length. Within fifteen miles of the coast are situated the remains of ten of the twelve cities of the Ionian confederacy, Miletus, Myus, Priene, Ephesus, Colophon, Lebedus, Teos, Erythræ, Clazomenæ and Phocaea; Samos and Chios, the two other members, were cities on the neighboring islands which bear their names. Many sites of other cities not members of the confederacy, and of centres of religious cults, are known all along the Ionian litoral and in the hills above the sea. To the north the Aegean shore extends 100 miles farther embracing Aeolis and the Troad, each with many important ancient sites. To the south lies Caria with still other remains of once powerful cities, and eastward, over the mountains, is ancient Lydia whose kings from time to time overcame the independent cities of the coast and controlled them.

And yet all this is only the fringe of Anatolia, a land which has known civilization from the almost forgotten days of the Hittites of the mainland and the Cretans of the sea, a land which saw the earliest beginnings of our own civilization, and figured prominently through the Hellenistic, Roman, and Byzantine periods, producing great men

[172]

and great works of art, through more than a thousand years, giving to the Christian church a number of its most renowned fathers, and bearing aloft the torch of civilization until it was overwhelmed by the Turks. Only a few spots, and not all of these the most important ones, in all that vast country with its hundreds of ancient sites, have as yet known the excavator's spade. A few of the ancient cities are now the sites of crowded Turkish towns. Most of them still conceal their historical and archaeological secrets, and their treasures of art, below the earth that has been accumulating for centuries. Turkish misrule which has been largely responsible for their ruin, has been responsible for the darkness which still enshrouds them. But it may be that a brighter day is dawning over ancient Anatolia.

Figure 3.—View in the Interior of the Theatre.

The traveller hardly knows which of the sites to visit among so great a number, and the archaeologist with permission to dig finds difficulty in deciding at which of the many unexplored places he would prefer to work. The traveller chooses the places which have been at least partly brought to light by the excavator. The excavator, on the other hand, looks for a site still buried, and as far away as possible from large modern towns; a site like Colophon which is so old as to have no history so late as Roman times, and so fortunate as to retain unchanged the Greek termination of its name.

Among the excavated, or partly excavated, cities of the coast district are Troy, Pergamum, Ephesus, Priene, Halicarnassus, Cnidus, Magnesia ad Maeandrum, Teos, Phocaea, and Didyma; in the interior only Boghaz Köi, the ancient Hittite Capital, Antioch of Pisidia, Sardis of Lydia and Gordium have known the excavator's spade.

Of these numerous sites, Ephesus, Pergamum, and Cnidus are described elsewhere in this number. Below are brief descriptions of Miletus, Priene and Sardis; the first an Ionian city of the first rank, the second a smaller member of the Ionian confederacy, and the third the capital of the Mermnad kings who were often the overlords of the cities of Ionia.

MILETUS.

Miletus held her place as the greatest Greek city until Hellenistic and Roman times when she was supplanted by Ephesus. Investigations at the site show that the city was flourishing in the later Minoan period. In the sixth century she peacefully owned the sway of the Lydian king Croesus, in the fourth she opposed Alexander; but eventually became a free Greek city again, and when Ionia came under Roman rule was a favored city of the emperors, particularly of Trajan.

The city lay on low land on the south shore of the Latmic gulf, not far from the open sea and a little below the mouth of the Maeander which in later centuries has filled up her port and made her an inland city. The river

Figure 4.—Seljuk Mosque at Miletus. (*Photograph by C. N. Read*)

flows today under her walls following the old line of the bay, and one approaches the modern town by a primitive ferry across the stream (Fig. 1). From the river one looks up to the ruins of the theatre, one of the largest in Asia, a structure of the Roman period built on older foundations. The city boasted no high acropolis of the form common in many Greek cities, though the hill against which the theatre was erected suggests one. The view of the theatre as seen from the river shows one of the great retaining walls of the *cavea*, or auditorium, with a large arched side entrance. Similar entrances appear on the face of these end walls (Fig. 2) on either hand. The walls are of marble exquisitely laid in late Hellenistic fashion, the arched entrances have rich face mouldings which are carried upon carved pilaster caps, and the stairs within, by which one mounted to the upper tiers of the seats are quite modern in proportions and design. There were fifty-four rows of seats divided into two tiers by a broad aisle, the lower tier still preserves its twenty rows of marble seats and the flights of steps which divide them, in almost perfect completeness (Fig. 3), and the substructures of the high Roman stage are quite well preserved. With so much of its marble facing still in place, this building at Miletus is one of the most beautiful of ancient theatres.

Passing from the theatre, in front of which there lie some very beautiful architectural details of the Hellenistic and Roman periods and several rather crude relief sculptures of animals, the visitor in search of remains of the ancient city encounters two difficulties which no doubt had been serious obstacles to the excavator, Dr. Theodor Wiegand, who laid bare a part of old Miletus under the auspices of the Berlin Academy. One of these difficulties is the proximity of a modern

[174]

Figure 5.—Entrance to the Mosque.

town of medium size which actually covers one of the most important parts of the Greek city, the other is the result of the silting up of the bay, and the consequent rising of the level of the river, which causes the deep excavations to be flooded throughout a good part of the year. The nearness of the town obstructs the view of the newly recovered ruins, and makes it necessary to barricade the excavations against the rapacity of the inhabitants for building materials, and the water usually prevents a thorough examination of the ruins. The water had very recently dried up in June 1914 when I last visited the place, and the lower parts of the marble buildings were covered with slimy mud. The excavators have found a Hellenistic agora, and near it a very interesting building, built somewhat like a small theatre and believed to be the Senate House. East of this is a large open space, like a huge atrium, surrounded by porticoes and enclosing a great altar of Artemis. Two temples were found, both existing in scant remains, one an archaic sanctuary of Artemis, the other dedicated to Apollo Delphinius.

Miletus is one of the few towns in western Asia Minor which preserves remnants of Seljuk art. The first wave of Turkish invaders differed from the later Ottoman conquerors of the country in that they were artists. The mosque here represented (Fig. 4) is a charming example of the work of these first Mohammedans to reach the Aegean. Constructed of excellent brick, and faced with white marble torn from Greek and Roman buildings, it presents no appearance of being patch-work. The tall octagonal base of the lofty dome is well proportioned to the cubical mass of the main body of the structure. The cornices and other carved mouldings are not fragments pieced together from the ruins of some Hellenistic building, but details of new Oriental patterns designed for their places. The windows are framed in richly carved

[175]

Figure 6.—View of Priene from the south, across the Maeander.

mouldings, and capped with diaper work of inlaid tiles in brilliant hues or intricate Arabic lettering once gilded upon coloured backgrounds. The triple-arched entrance is executed in marbles of various colours, and abounds in richly wrought mouldings, intricate diaper-work and open work grilles of marble executed with incredible delicacy. (Fig. 5.) The tomb in front of the Mosque is an example of later Turkish art.

PRIENE

Between Miletus and Priene once spread out the blue waters of the Latmic Gulf; but the ever-busy Maeander has converted the bay into a plain, so that one now travels from one city to the other over moist fields and reedy marshes, crossing and recrossing the windings of the river many times on his direct march. Miletus was larger, richer, and more powerful than Priene; but Priene looked down upon Miletus.

Poised upon her lofty crag, a spur of giant Mycale which rises behind her to the north, the little city held one of the most imposing and most beautiful situations in the world of her time, looking south over the gulf at her feet, beyond Miletus, Pyrrha and Myus, to the highlands of Caria, and westward far out over the Aegean.

As the traveller of today approaches the high-perched city, deserted now these many centuries, a view is presented to him not unlike that which greeted travellers in ships in ancient times (Fig. 6). The same walls stand out boldly from their rocky slope, the terraces upon which the city's buildings still stand in ruins, rise one above the other surmounted by the lofty platform of Athena's temple, all ascending like giant steps toward the pinnacle of the high acropolis. It is not difficult from a distance, to restore the outlines of the marble buildings, and, in imagination to repopulate the streets, the

[176]

Figure 7.—Terrace of the Temple, from a street below.

walls, and the agora, with living men and women.

The early history of Priene is unknown. The city was destroyed by Ardys, King of Lydia, in the seventh century; but soon recovered, and, in the middle of the sixth, reached the zenith of its career. Having fallen to Cyrus in 545, it passed under Persian sway, until set free by Alexander the Great who became a generous patron of the city. Hard times came upon Priene after Alexander's death; the kings of Pergamum and Cappadocia threatened her from two sides and she was saved eventually by the Romans in 155 B.C. The city flourished under Roman rule and was a place of some importance under the Byzantine empire.

Priene has been thoroughly excavated. In this case too Dr. Wiegand was in charge of the work. But the absence of a modern town, and the height and dryness of the situation made the site a far easier and pleasanter one to uncover than Miletus. The excavations brought to light the most complete example in existence of an ancient Greek town, most of its remains belonging to the period of rebuilding in the fourth and third centuries B.C. Priene is often called the Pompeii of the Greek world, and indeed, certain views of its residential quarters suggest the victim of Vesuvius. Though built up on terraces on a steep hillside, the town was laid out with great regularity, having six main avenues and fifteen narrower streets; all paved and provided with side-walk and gutters, dividing the city into rectangles. Besides the beautiful temple of Athena Polias situated on a high broad platform (Fig. 7) the city boasted a number of less important sanctuaries, a fine colonnaded marketplace surrounded with shops and public buildings, a smaller market in which fish and meat were sold, a theatre, an assembly hall and two gymnasia. Practically all the buildings which we see today are remains of the fourth and third centuries before Christ. The scant remains of the temple of Athena

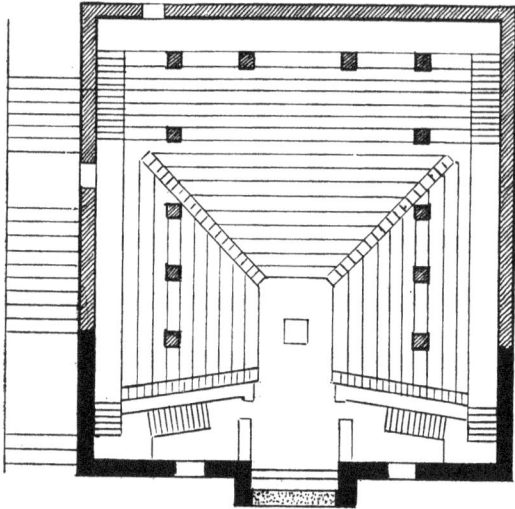

PRIENE· EKKLESIASTERION·
Figure 8.

which were standing when the site was examined by the Society of the Dilettanti in 1765 and 1868, have all but disappeared, having been taken to embellish European museums, and we now find only a few broken, but very beautiful, architectural fragments lying upon the smooth white surface of the temple platform. Before the temple stood the great altar, still plainly visible in its ruins, and, to the east of this, the Propylaea, one of the later embellishments of the temple precinct. A fine flight of about fifty marble steps, with buildings enclosing it on either hand, descends to the northwest angle of the great agora. Through this fine marble-paved marketplace passes the principal east-and-west street of the city. Along the north side of the street, facing the agora, extends a long double colonnade set upon a sort of terrace of several steps above the level of the pavement. This fine structure was about 350 feet long. Its rear wall, throughout the greater part of its length, is filled with doorways which

open upon small chambers like shops; but near the east end the stoa fronts upon the ecclesiasterion or assembly hall which is one of the best preserved and most interesting of ancient Greek civic buildings. It has the general form of a theatre, but is square instead of curved. (Fig 8.) A square space with a beautiful little altar in the middle occupies the place of the orchestra. From this the tiers of carved seats rise on three sides in straight lines (Fig. 9) and have steps at the angles and at the ends. At the top is a broad aisle. Square marble piers were placed at intervals along the sides and across the rear which probably helped to support a roof. At the back an upper tier of seats rises higher than at the sides. In front of this, occupying the place of the stage in a theatre, is a rectangular exedra with carved benches on three sides—the seats of the mighty. On either hand is a doorway leading out upon the great colonnade, and at the back of the exedra is a broad arch, still partly preserved, which provided a wide semicircular opening forming a sort of window above the bench of the presiding officers. This arch, with another which spans the east entrance to the agora, is one of the earliest examples of arch construction in Greek architecture.

The other sides of the agora are provided with colonnades of columns in a single row, behind which are little shops, and on the east is the straight rear wall of the sanctuary of Asclepius. The open square is dotted with larger and smaller bases for statues, marble exedras, and honorific stelae.

In another part of the city, high up to the north, against the steep hill-side, is the little theatre, one of the most interesting of all the smaller theatres of the old Greek world. Only the

Figure 9.—Interior of the Ecclesiasterion, or Assembly Hall.

lower rows of its seats (Fig. 10) with five carved thrones in the lowest row, remain of the *koilon*, or auditorium; but the stage building preserves enough of its colonnaded front (Fig. 10) to have aroused once more, without definitely settling, the long-disputed controversy as to whether the Greek players stood upon a raised platform or upon the orchestra level. A row of piers with engaged columns of the Doric order carried a light entablature and a set of stone beams, like a roof-structure, providing a narrow shelf, about 12 feet high and 9 feet wide which some authorities would have us believe was the actual stage.

From every point of vantage in the ruins one looks down upon the residential parts of the city which the excavators have uncovered. It is amazing to see the checker-board plan of squares of private houses, divided by straight white streets well paved and drained, quite as regularly laid out upon the uneven slope as if upon a flat

plain. The houses are built of stone, not infrequently of marble, on the Greek plan with open court, columned porch and living rooms large and small, four residences to a block or *insula*. (Fig. 11.)

The stadium and gymnasium were built in the lowest section of the city, within the walls, just above the sea level, and a long flight of steps descended to them from the marketplace. The stadium was a curious structure with banks of seats on one side only, the other being open toward the bay. In front of the seats, the actual floor of the stadium was an artificial terrace held up by a high, stout retaining wall. Behind the seats ran a long covered portico. The gymnasium joined onto the stadium at the west. Like other Greek buildings of its kind, it consisted of an open colonnaded court with halls and smaller rooms on two sides. In the lavatory one still may see a row of large marble wash-basins along the wall, below a moulding which carries

Figure 10.—End of seats and part of stage building in the Theatre of Priene.

a water conduit and is pierced with openings masked by well carved lions' heads, one to each basin (Fig. 12); all so well preserved as to give a sense of living reality to this place in which the youth of Priene exercised and played, and contended in their sports over two thousand years ago.

SARDIS.

A traveller in ancient times, wishing to travel from one of the coast cities of Ionia inland to the great Lydian capital, would probably have gone first to Ephesus, and from that city would have followed the great highway, or Royal Road, over the mountains, out into the plain of the Hermus, and along the south side of that plain to the ancient city of the Mermnadae which sat astride the great trade route and beside the gold-bearing sands of the Pactolus, a little less than a hundred miles from Ephesus. Modern travellers would find the journey over the mountains both long and tedious. The railway from Smyrna avoids the mountains, making a long detour along the bay, and finally entering the valley near the mouth of the Hermus. As the site of Sardis is approached one observes, away toward the north across the river, a group of conical tumuli of various sizes, two of them appearing as large as the great pyramid of Egypt. These are the famous tombs of the Lydian kings, described by Herodotus. On the opposite side of the railway extends a long range of tall crags and pinnacles rising out of the edge of the plain against a dark background formed by the masses of the snow-capped Boz-Dagh, Mt. Tmolus, the legendary birthplace of Bacchus. These crags and pinnacles are made of deep red clay, and erosion has given them their fantastic architectural forms. One of them turns out to be the acropolis of ancient Sardis (Fig. 13). Fragments of walls are balanced about its crumbling crest and half buried ruins of late Roman buildings cluster around its foot. The earliest historical

[180]

ART AND ARCHAEOLOGY

Figure 11.—Group of Houses.

references show that this acropolis was in existence in the eighth or ninth century before Christ, and it is probable that the place was a stronghold in far more distant antiquity. The hill now terminates in a sharp ridge by no means large enough to have held the upper city and the fortifications described by the early writers. It is plain that the acropolis, like the hills on either side of it, has been worn away by erosion to its present shape. There are no remnants of the early walls, the present ones having been made in Byzantine times out of marble blocks and other fragments taken from Greek and Roman buildings (Fig. 14). But this is actually the remnant of the hill which was rendered impregnable, before the dawn of history, by King Meles who, by direction of the oracle at Telmessus, carried a lion around its walls. It is the hill unsuccessfully besieged by the Cimmerians in the earliest historical period, lost by Croesus to the Persians, regained by Alexander, and treacherously betrayed under Achaeus. It is a matter of historical record that the city of Sardis was destroyed by earthquake in A.D. 17, and it is probable that part of the acropolis collapsed in that catastrophe. It is evident that the hill

has been rapidly disintegrating ever since, and the washing away of its fabric has buried the lower city, between it and the Pactolus.

The excavation of the ancient city has been undertaken by an American society. Work was begun in the early spring of 1910 and carried on, at periods of five months in each year, until the summer of 1914. The area covered by the city is very extensive, on the north and west of the acropolis and on both sides of the Pactolus. A beginning was made at the river-side on the west of the hill, at a point where two large Ionic columns protruded half their height above a field of barley (Fig. 15). At the end of five campaigns, a temple of Artemis of colossal dimensions, had been brought to light (Fig. 16). This temple, all of marble brought from quarries on the side of Mt. Tmolus, was begun in the fourth century, or perhaps

Figure 14.—Walls of Acropolis, view from the south.

earlier, on the site of an old temple destroyed by fire during the Ionian revolt in 506 B.C. It was roofed, and certainly in use, before the end of the century, and was repaired in later centuries as the remains show. The problem of excavation was a difficult one; owing partly to the depth of the

Figure 12.—Lavatory in the Gymnasium.

accumulated earth and débris, which rose from twelve feet at the west end to sixty at a point east of the building; this latter being by far the greatest depth for excavations yet undertaken in this part of the world. But the temple proved to be preserved almost exactly in proportion as it was deeply buried, and now stands free as one of the best preserved of the Greek temples in Asia Minor (Fig. 16). Its plan shows that there were eight column at the ends and twenty on the sides, the porches were deep with interior

Figure 13.—Valley of the Pactolus, Acropolis of Sardis on the left and Mt. Tmolus behind.
(*Photograph by D. M. Robinson*)

Figure 15.—General view of the American excavations at Sardis, view from the west.

Figure 16.—The Temple of Artemis, view from the east.

Figure 17.—The East Porch of the Temple, view from the north.

Figure 18.—The East Porch of the Temple, view from the south.

columns unusually arranged. The cella was composed of a long chamber divided by two rows of five columns each, and a treasury chamber; this latter has a long inscription in Greek—a mortgage—upon its walls. As seen from the north or south (Figs. 17 and 18), the east porch of the temple, with its two complete columns and thirteen others which preserve half their original height, with its projecting anta walls, its portal standing to one third of its original height, and numerous interesting details lying about, presents an effect of spacious dignity. Some of the carved details are unusually beautiful, particularly some of the capitals which were discovered deep down in the earth.

East of the temple, with its front wall almost touching the two columns at the south end of the east row, a little Christian church was unearthed (Fig. 15). It is built of brick and is of oblong plan with a small apse at its east end perfectly preserved. Outside the small apse is a larger apse, the half dome of which has fallen in. Coins of the third and fourth centuries were found in the cracks of the pavement. The little building is interesting in view of the reference of St. John in the Revelation to a church community at Sardis.

Many fragments of sculpture were found in the process of excavation, and a lion figure of the Lydian period resting upon a stepped base together with a second lion, much mutilated, and an eagle, all in marble. Among the sculptures which have been found representing the best period of Greek art in Sardis is the spirited head of a horse.

Of great scientific importance was the discovery here of an unknown language in a large body of inscriptions in the tongue and script of the ancient Lydians. The finding of a bilingual inscription, that is, an inscription in the unknown Lydian with a translation in Aramaic, has made important progress toward the deciphering of this new language. Simultaneous digging carried on in the old necropolis across the river from the temple has brought to light a vast number of objects of daily use in the life of the ancient Lydians, objects which shed much light upon the state of civilization to which this great non-Hellenic kingdom had attained, and many of them are of unusual beauty. Among the various classes of objects are pottery of new shapes and designs, bronze utensils and other objects, terra cottas, ivories, silver ware, coins, gold ornaments and engraved gems. Among the terra-cottas are mask-like figures in archaic style, showing the entire front of the body above the waist, and preserving beautiful colour designs, and figurines of many types, some plainly from the Myrina manufactories, others of types quite new. Although these excavations were hardly more than begun when the war put a stop to further progress on the work, enough material has been recovered to afford a very good foundation for restoring the civilization of ancient Lydia.

Princeton University.

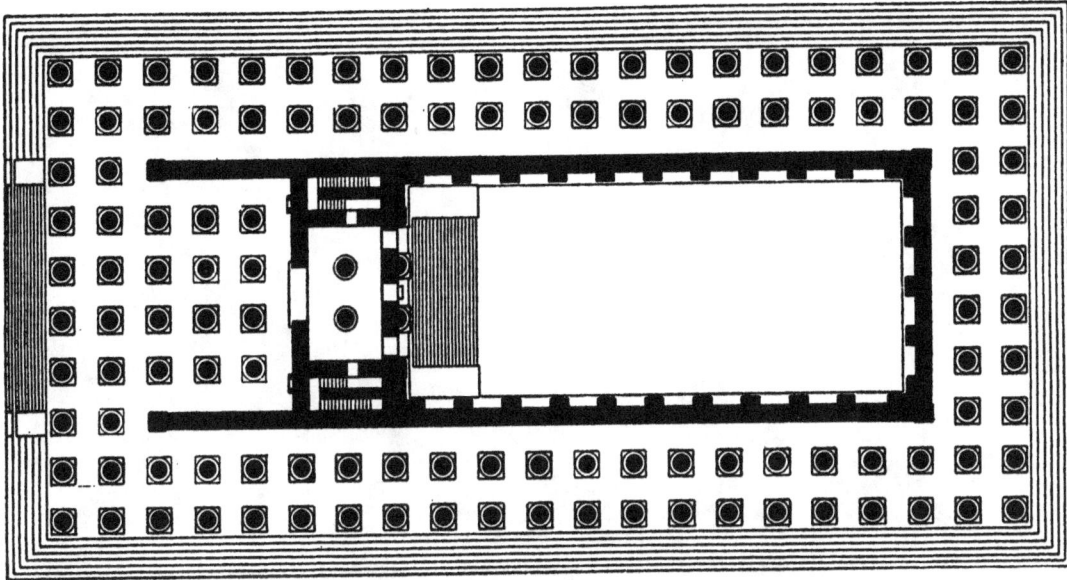

Figure 1.—Plan of Didymaeum (*after Wiegand*).

DIDYMA

By E. Baldwin Smith

GREATEST of all religious edifices erected by Greek antiquity," writes Strabo, "is the Didymaeum." Great it was, though not actually the largest in size. Still it was not alone the tradition of its dimensions which inspired Vitruvius to rank it among the four great temples of antiquity, and second only to the Artemisium. Its architectural fame must have rested, to a large extent, upon those unique and ambitious features of its construction which made it so radically different from all other Greek temples.

Before investigating the fascinating and rather baffling mysteries of the actual temple, the reader, like a visitor to the famous site, must, even at the expense of some wearisome moments, make his geographical and historical approach to the prophetic shrine of the Ionians. The temple, dedicated to Apollo, was built by the people of Miletus, in their own territory, about ten miles south of their city on the promontory of Poseideion, at Didyma, which is today the flourishing little Turkish town of Hieronta. Didyma, in ancient times, was often called Branchidae, after the priestly caste who guarded the treasures of the temple, ministered to the oracle, and were supposed to have descended from Branchus the youth beloved of Apollo.

During Greek times Didyma was inaccessible by land, even from the mother city Miletus, and was always approached by sea. The principal port was Panormus where landed all the pilgrims from the Mediterranean world who sought guidance of the prophetic utterances at the shrine of Apollo. From Panormus to the sanctuary runs a Sacred Way, in length about a mile and a half, which was flanked on either side by huge, archaic, seated statues of the former worshipers. This Sacred

Figure 2.—East end of Temple.

Way, with its ponderous and rough-hewn statues, recalls the sacred avenues of sphinxes which led from the Nile to the great Egyptian temples, and suggests, as does the general type of the seated figures, the influence of Nilotic art upon the Milesians. It was not until Roman times, under the Emperor Hadrian, that an actual road was built connecting Didyma with Miletus.

There was an ancient Ionic temple of Apollo at Didyma which was destroyed. While the first Artemisium was not burnt until the night of Alexander's birth according to ancient legend, the earliest Didymaeum, after having first been plundered by the Persian Darius in 494, was finally sacked and burnt to the ground by Xerxes in 481 B.C. During one or the other of these devastating inroads the celebrated bronze statue of Apollo by Canachus was removed to the Persian capital at Susa, taking with it much of the prophetic fame of the shrine. It is a sad story, the sack of the first Didymaeum, if we can believe the story which has come down to us, that the hereditary priestly caste of the Branchidae betrayed the temple's riches to Xerxes, as he was returning from his ill-fated expedition against the Greeks, and then went into voluntary exile beyond the river Oxus to escape the vengeance of the outraged Milesians. It was there, beyond the Oxus, that Alexander the Great found their descendants in 328, and exter-

[188]

The actual work commenced in 333 B.C. and, if we can be sure that Vitruvius was describing the second and not the first Didymeaum, the architects were Daphnis and Paeonius, the builder of the Artemisium at Ephesus. Either the conception of these architects was too ambitious or the times too rife with war, for the work languished, lapsed, and was revived periodically for several centuries, without the colossal temple ever having been entirely completed. While the temple was left gableless and unfinished, the last work having ceased apparently in 41 A.D., it was nevertheless in use, and was considered one of the greatest monuments of antiquity and excited the admiration of all the Roman writers on architecture, including Vitruvius, Strabo, Pliny, and Pausanias.

Figure 3.—Great Portal at east end (*after Wiegand*).

minated them, men, women, and children, as punishment for the sins of their fore-fathers.

For about a century the Milesians seem to have been either unable to rebuild the temple or to have felt it useless to restore a shrine from which the famous cultus statue of the god has been removed. Therefore, it was not until the year 333 B. C., at the request of Alexander, that the work of erecting a new structure was commenced. Perhaps the Macedonian chieftain promised that the cultus statue would be rescued from the barbarians and returned, as soon as a suitable sanctuary should be ready for its reception. Whether or not such a promise stimulated the people of Miletus to revive the prestige of their shrine by a new and even greater monument, we know that in 295 B.C. Seleucus I, did restore the sacred image to the new temple.

Figure 4.—One of side entrances at east end (*after Wiegand*).

Figure 5.—Cella, looking west.

Even now our approach to the temple is not entirely cleared, for its mysteries are only in part those of incantation and mystic divination. For centuries a veil of mystery and uncertainty has hung over the whole architectural character of the building, with the result that no text book or work on architecture has been published containing a plan of the temple which gives an accurate or adequate idea of the unparalleled features of this unique monument of Hellenistic Greek architecture. The reason why the students of architecture have had such erroneous conceptions of the building is easily explicable and excusable, and can be accounted for by a brief survey of the European investigation of the Didymaeum.

The darkness which closed over the ancient world during the Middle Ages, and which enveloped the Didymaeum along with all the other works of classical antiquity, was lifted, in the case of

the Apollo temple, in 1446, when Cyriac of Ancona visited the site and described the greater part of the temple as still standing, although the *cella* had been converted into a fortress by the Byzantines. Upon the arrival of the next recorded visitor, the Englishman Dr. Pickering, in 1673, the temple was found to have collapsed, due probably to the great earthquake of 1493. In 1764 and 1812 the Society of Dilettanti sent expeditions to explore the ruins, and in 1873, the "Rothschild Expedition" under MM. O. Rayet and A. Thomas, visited the site, sent certain sculptures to the Louvre, and published "Milet et le Golfe Latmique" with a plan of the temple which was largely conjectural. No excavations, however, were made until 1895 when Haussoullier and Pontremoli visited the site and cleared the western façade, and part of the east front, but had to limit their excavations to the outskirts of the

[190]

Figure 6.—Cella, looking east.

temple because they found that the Turkish village had encroached upon the ruins and had established a formidable wind-mill immediately above the heart of the temple. With the new material they had uncovered, with the inscriptions pertaining to the work, and with the results from pits sunk in various parts of the ruins, the French expedition published its results under the title "Didymes." Their plan, however, failed to disclose the exact nature of the innovations of the strange edifice. In 1905 the French rights were ceded to Dr. Th. Wiegand, the German excavator of Miletus, who proceeded to clear the whole temple and remove the inconvenient wind-mill. The full revelation of this uncovering is even yet unpublished, although in 1911 Dr.

Wiegand published a report of the work made before the Prussian Academy of Sciences, in which were an almost correct plan of the building and some very interesting photographs. The illustrations in this article are taken from his report, with the addition of other unpublished pictures taken by Professor Howard Crosby Butler after the site was cleared.

Turning now to the actual temple and approaching it, as the ancient pilgrim did, along the Sacred Way, the road leads one into the sacred precinct on the north side, so that the visitor has to pass down the temple to the left before the great entrance on the east is reached (Fig. 1). The precinct was a walled enclosure, semicircular at either end, and, from its form and from the remains of banks of seats on the south side, recalls a *stadion*, or race-track, which Dr. Wiegand declares the site originally to have been.

The temple itself is in the Ionic order, is decastyle, dipteral, has twenty-one columns on a side, and has three rows of four columns in antis on the east end. Translating this cryptic description into plain English, the temple is surrounded by a continuous colonnade of two rows of columns, ten across the east and west ends and twenty-one down each side; at the east end there is a recess between the cella walls which is filled with twelve columns in three rows of four columns each.

The whole structure rests upon a seven stepped platform, or *crepidoma*, and measures, along the edge of the top step, in length about 360 feet and in width about 163 feet. Being of such gigantic size, the steps, as is the custom in classical architecture, are scaled to the building, and are too high for comfortable approach. Therefore the actual approach on the east front is by means of thirteen smaller steps extending along the front of the temple between the third column from each side and flanked by parotids on either side. These parotids, as the photograph shows (Fig. 2), are unfinished and were intended to have been carved and decorated. Having ascended the crepidoma, the visitor is confronted by an avenue of vast columns which leads into what is usually called the *pronaos*, which is here a *dodecastylon*, or portico of twelve columns, and then brings up at what might naturally be expected to be the main entrance of the temple. At this point the idiosyncrasies of the Didymaeum commence. The inscriptions of the workmen, found in the temple, speak of the ante-room with the twelve columns not as a *pronaos* but as a *prodomos*,

the reason being, no doubt, because it is not actually *pro naos*, as another chamber interposes between it and the naos where the image of the god was enshrined. In addition to the change of name, this prodomos is unlike any pronaos in Greek architecture in its wilderness of vast columns. We are accustomed to two, or even three columns *in antis*, but to find as many as twelve suggests only a Persian *apadana* or an Egyptian hypostyle hall.

The greatest surprise, however, awaits the visitor at the end of the *prodomos*, at what should be the main portal of the sanctuary. Here is the huge portal, as is to be expected, with remains of its carefully carved door-jambs; but what of the door-sill! It is over six feet high with no steps leading up to it, and evidence, in its carefully executed and carved torus and scotia mouldings which carry out the base mouldings of the cella wall (Fig. 3), that no steps were ever intended to ascend it. Where then was the entrance? At either side of the main portal, almost next to the side walls of the *prodomos*, are doorways (Fig. 4), flanked on each side by pilasters, and capped by huge rough quarried lintels whose faces were intended to be carved. These doorways give access to long, descending ramps roofed at first by deep coffers and then by beautifully cut arches, one of the earliest, if not the first, example of the Greek use of the arch. These ramps, in descending, pass under the chamber which lies between the *prodomos* and the *naos*, under a long flight of steps which lead back up from the *naos* to this chamber, and out into the actual cella which was unroofed and sunk far below the outer level of the temple. The floor of the cella is about 14 feet below the top of the *crepidoma*, and on all sides appears to consist of a high,

Figure 7.—Columns of Peristyle on northeast corner.

twenty-foot podium, or platform, from which the walls rise, broken at intervals by strong, salient pilasters (Fig. 5). At the west end of the cella was the adyton or covered shrine of Canachus' Apollo.

Standing now in the cella, and looking back towards the east, the visitor is confronted by another striking structural feature of the building. A long, broad, and majestic flight of twenty-two steps, about 53.25 feet wide and 19.66 feet deep, leads up to the chamber under which one enters the cella. At the top of the steps are three doorways, the central one being flanked by two half columns, of the same scale as those on the exterior of the building, which are supposed to have been capped by Corinthian instead of Ionic capitals (Fig. 6).

Passing through any one of the three doorways it is discovered that the level of this chamber is almost flush with the top of the sill of the main portal opening into the *prodomos*. In other words, its level is about six feet above the top of the crepidoma. Within, at either side of the center of this room, two columns without plinths, and of a scale slightly smaller than the exterior columns, are placed as supports to the now vanished ceiling. This chamber, from inscriptions found within its ruins, was called by the builders the *chresmographion*, or the place of the writing of the oracles. It was therefore the business office of the temple. On each side of this *chresmographion* a door opens upon a flight of stairs which ascends, in two stages, to a sort of room which, in all probability, included only the small space above the stairs and in height was about equal to one half the height of the *chresmographion*. The ceiling of these stairs has a very remarkable square-and-key fret very deeply cut into the stone. From the inscriptions we again learn that these storied side-chambers, with their broken flights of stairs, were called labyrinths. It is likely that they gave access to the storerooms of the temple where the treasures and entrusted riches were guarded, and where the *prytanes*, the officials of the oracle, kept their records. Every Greek temple, besides accumulating vast riches of its own, functioned as the forefather of the modern bank, guarding the wealth intrusted to its care, and loaning out money at interest on safe collateral. The absence, then, of the *opisthodomos*, or treasury, at the west end of the temple, makes it necessary to accept the second story as the banking quarters of the Branchidae priests and their more honest successors.

The architectural and sculptural forms of the Didymaeum, while in many cases unfinished and for the most part of relatively late date in the history of Greek architecture, present a variety

DIDYMES

Figure 8.—Entablature of Didymaeum (*after Haussoullier and Pontremoli*).

and inventiveness in harmony with the original and ambitious plan of the temple. The great columns of the peristyle, huge channelled shafts of sixty feet in height (Fig. 7), have, with the exception of the outer row across the east end, the typical bases of the Hellenistic period, consisting of a torus moulding, with horizontal channellings, resting upon two scotia which in turn are supported by a square plinth block. Across the front of the temple the bases of the eight central columns of the exterior row are each different in the forms of their mouldings and are richly carved with various ornamental motives. While they are all set upon plinth blocks, the bases of the two central columns have, instead of the traditional torus, a flat band of sculpture, consisting of alternating palmettes and anthemions, resting upon a double scotia. Other bases of this row have anthemions carved upon the toruses, and frets carved upon circular plinths which take the place of scotias, while one base, near the center of the façade, has a torus decorated with vertical water leaves, raised upon a twelve-sided plinth, each face of which is sculptured with a different conventional floral motive.

Regarding the Ionic capitals of the columns, as in the case of the whole superstructure of the temple, the question becomes somewhat conjectural due to the devastation of time, man, and the elements. The three capitals, which are still in place on their tall shafts, are rather depressed and late, but perfectly ordinary examples of Hellenistic work. Among the ruins of the façade were found fragments from which a peculiar and very interesting capital has been reconstructed and which is illustrated here from the restoration of Haussoullier and Pontremoli (Fig. 8). Instead of the spiral volutes, it has the busts of Apollo and Zeus, one on either face, the sculptured heads recalling most suggestively the influence of the Pergamene School of sculpture as it appears on the Great Altar of Zeus at Pergamum which belongs to the second century B.C. In the center of the capital, in place of the echinus of eggs, is a salient head of a bull, beneath which is a band of palmettes and anthemions. Other fragments found among the débris of the temple suggest as great a variety of capitals across the east façade of the temple as there are bases, although the two examples already described are the only ones sufficiently well preserved to permit of restoration.

The entablature, as restored from the fragments by Haussoullier and Pontremoli, shows a very late and ornate treatment; its interesting features are the heavy dentils whose faces are each carved with a different motive, and the heavy acanthus rinceau, with a Medusa head in the Pergamene style, carved upon the frieze. Beyond the entablature it is impossible to go in the reconstruction of the temple, for as Strabo says, the temple was so large that it had no roof, and excavations have shown that it was left unfinished and probably without even a gabled pediment at the east end. Within the cella there are some exquisite pilaster capitals which are much more vigorous and pleasing than any fragments which remain from the exterior of the temple, and suggest an early period in the erection of the sanctuary. The fact that after nearly five hundred years the temple was unfinished does not seem to have lessened its glory and fame in the eyes of classical writers, and, when its remains are finally published, its greatness, as the most picturesque temple of antiquity, may once more be fully appreciated.

Princeton University.

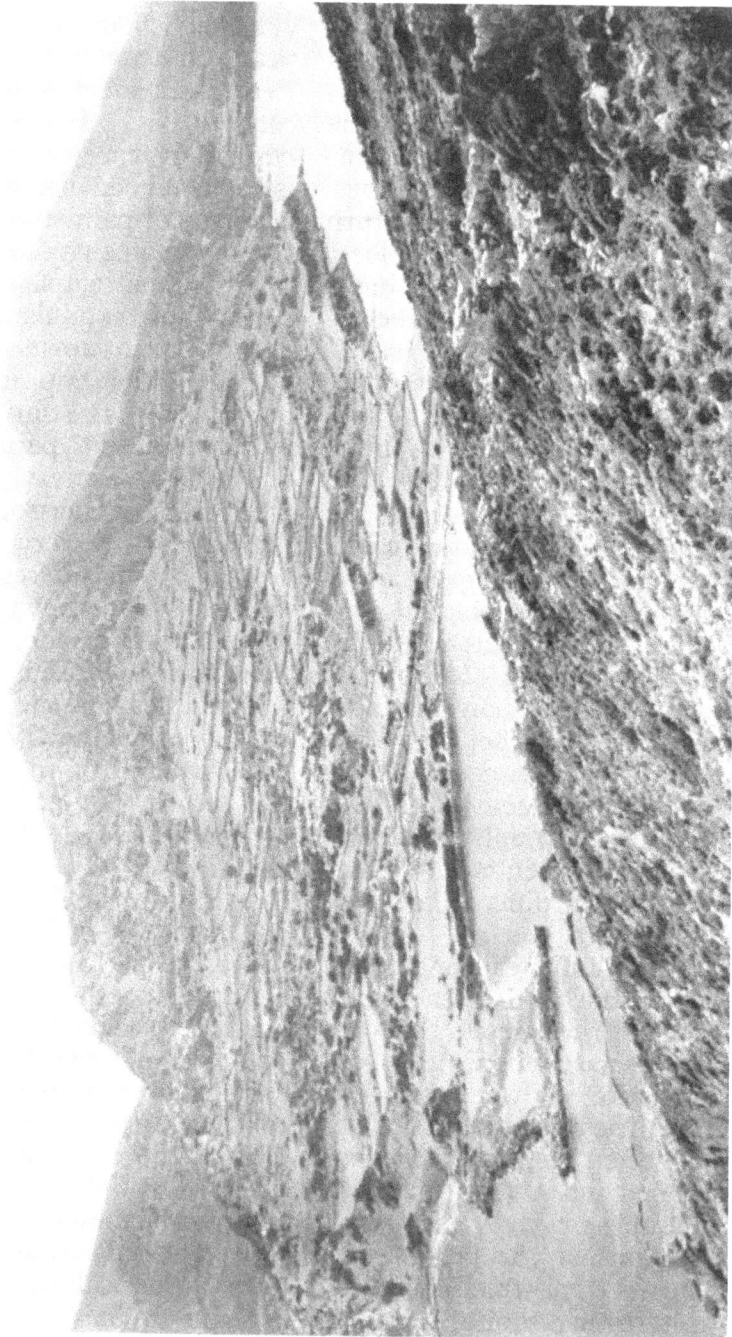

Figure 1.—Acropolis of Cnidus and site of city from southwest.

CNIDUS

By T. Leslie Shear

A VISITOR to Caria in southwestern Asia Minor, who stands on the hills of the Dorian peninsula, "whence Cnidus, light of Caria, is revealed," sees spread out before him a varied and noble panorama. Nature has been lavish in endowing with beauty the islands and coasts of the Aegean, but here at the steep and rugged point where the cold waters of the north meet the southern waves she seems to have lingered with peculiar fondness. The lofty range of mountains which constitutes the peninsula is terminated at the west by a high hill that is isolated from its range by a deep-cleft valley. This hill is the acropolis of the city and by its very nature justifies the descriptive epithet applied to Cnidus in the earliest reference to the city in Greek literature, the Homeric Hymn to Apollo, where mention is made of "lofty Cnidus." On the east a sharp spur, at right angles to the acropolis, runs to the sea, and the goodly space bounded by these hills and washed on the other sides by the waters of the sea is a natural and inevitable site for a city. (Fig. 1.)

The climate here is unusually salubrious, as the heat of summer is always tempered by a cooling breeze, and in winter the southern sun rarely hides his face. A refreshing fountain still gurgles in the ruins and occasional rains revive the drooping trees. The city's nearest neighbors are the island of Nisyrus on the south and the island of Cos on the west, the latter famous as the home of Hippocrates and the centre of medical lore for the ancient world, the former still a Mecca for invalids in quest of its healing sulphur baths. Cnidus, too, had part in this culture of medicine and hygiene and made full contribution to the medical cause in giving to the world the renowned historian and physician Ctesias.

Terrace upon terrace, street after street, buildings innumerable, still even in their ruin impress the visitor with the extent and magnificence of the city. We wonder at her wealth when we think of the famous treasury and paintings dedicated by her at Delphi; we admire her taste when we look upon copies of the Aphrodite of Praxiteles; we recognize her engineering skill in the attempt to cut a canal through the peninsula at Bybassus. But thwarted in this engineering project, subjugated by Persia and humbled by the loss of her walls, the city subsequently sought to steer a neutral course in the quarrels of her neighbors. The larger harbor was the rendezvous of Cimon's fleet in 466 B.C., and for years the city paid tribute to Athens, though in 394 B.C. when Conon defeated the Spartans in the naval battle of Cnidus, the place was held by the Lacedaemonians.

On a headland just east of the harbor, conspicuous far and near, by land and sea, especially glorious in the sunset light, when the nearer point gleams gold against a burning red, stand the ruins of a lofty monument, once crowned by a colossal lion. Sir Charles Newton, in 1858, carried this lion to London, where it now adorns the British Museum, and since Newton's time there has been general acceptance of his

Figure 2.—Points east of harbour of Cnidus. On the most distant stood the Lion Monument.

theory that this monument was erected in commemoration of the naval victory of Conon. (Fig. 2.)

Newton made scattered excavations in the city in the spring of 1858 and was so fortunate as to discover and transport safely to England the noble marble statue, usually known as the Demeter of Cnidus. (Fig. 3.) Thus we have evidence that the city fostered the fine arts rather than developed military science. And though her walls were rebuilt, by Alexander's permission, so massively that they are visible to-day throughout their entire circuit, yet the city's chief accomplishment in the fourth century was the purchase from Praxiteles of a statue of Aphrodite. The sculptor offered to the people of Cos the choice of two statues of Aphrodite, one of which was draped, the other nude. The Coans made their selection

and the undraped statue fell to Cnidus, which thenceforward became the shrine for worshippers of beauty throughout the world. (Fig 4.)

Who has not drifted languidly on a smiling sea, with Lucian and his friends into that welcoming harbor, and passed through the busy streets of the city, noticing, perhaps, on one side the stoa of Sostratus, on the other, may be, the observatory of Eudoxus, or other temples and public buildings, ultimately to come to the precinct and temple of Aphrodite of the Fair Winds? The grounds about the temple were richly planted with groves and gardens, with flower and vine, affording delightful places of resort for votaries of Aphrodite on her festal days. Within the temple the Goddess herself greeted one with a benignant smile. Impossi-

[198]

Figure 3.—"Demeter," from Cnidus, in the British Museum.

Figure 4.—Walls on northwest end of Acropolis of Cnidus.

ble is a description of the beauty revealed and only its effects are recorded.

When reading Lucian it is difficult to believe that he is describing a visit now eighteen centuries past; when roaming over the ruins of Cnidus it seems incredible that we can not conjure back the Goddess and her temple. Yet we know full well that Aphrodite of Cnidus was long since burned in Constantinople, and that no trace of her temple has been found.

Newton dug occasional holes, here and there, within the city's walls, and was richly rewarded for his pains, but as a whole the city is lying beneath the dust of ages in beautiful isolation, rarely visited except by the shepherd and his sheep, waiting until in the fulness of time the archaeologist shall shall again uncover its streets and squares, reveal and reconstruct its temples and its homes.

Columbia University.

[200]

CURRENT NOTES AND COMMENTS

Notes from the National Gallery

THE National Gallery of Art has just received through the State Department, as a gift from the Duchess of Marlborough and other American born English friends of this country, a full length statue in white marble of Lord Chatham. It is by Francis Derwent Wood, a Royal Academician. The pedestal of gray marble is inscribed as follows: "This statue of William Pitt, Earl of Chatham, the British champion of American liberty, is presented by American women living in the United Kingdom as a memorial of the one hundred years peace between the two kindred nations and as an expression of their love for the land of their birth, and the land of their adoption. 1815–1915."

Two important canvasses, "Evening Tide, California," by William Ritschel, and "Gray Day," by W. Granville Smith, have just been added to the National Gallery collection. They were acquired through purchase by the Ranger fund in accordance with a provision of the will of Henry W. Ranger, recently deceased. A fund of some $200,000 left to the National Academy of Design; the income to be used for purchasing paintings by American artists; the pictures to be given to art institutions in America maintaining public galleries; and this upon the express condition that the National Gallery shall have the option and right to take, reclaim, and own any picture so purchased by the Academy. The gallery has also received a very charming replica of Power's Greek Slave, the gift of Mrs. B. H. Warder.

King Solomon's Mines

The Arts Club of Washington on March 25, 1920 had an illustrated lecture by Courtenay De Kalb, Mining Engineer, just returned from making a special investigation of the mineral industry in Spain, Portugal, and Morocco for the Department of Commerce, on "A Visit to Some of King Solomon's Mines." Following generally accepted views of European, and especially Spanish, scholars, Mr. De Kalb identifies Spain with the Biblical Tarshish. Tartessus was probably a name derived from Tarshish. It included the whole of the valley of the Guadalquivir, the adjacent territory now politically separated as the province of Huelva, and seems to have included the east coast of Spain on account of the trade with the interior from the mart of Saguntum, now called Sagunto. Ezekiel mentions Tarshish as the source of silver, iron, tin and lead. Elsewhere in the Bible copper is added to the list of these resources. The copper and silver came chiefly from what are today the pyrite mines of Huelva, the principal mines being called the "Rio Tinto" and the "Tharsis." Remains of an ancient Phoenician furnace have been found at Rio Tinto, and the slag-piles of the Phoenicians and Romans at this single mine exceed 13,000,000 tons, representing an estimated output of 2,500,000 tons of copper and 700,000,000 ounces of silver. A son of King Solomon is said to have lived in a castle, the remains of which exist upon the summit of the peak called Cerro de Salomón, overlooking the mines today. This is possible, since the representatives of Solomon went wherever the joint operations of Solomon and Hiram extended throughout the then known world. A

ART AND ARCHAEOLOGY

tomb has been reported as being discovered among the ruins of the rich archaeological site of Sagunto which bore an inscription stating that Adoniram, collector of tribute for King Solomon was buried there. The site of Saguntum, with its magnificent ruins, has never been the subject of archaeological investigation except in so far as was possible without the assistance of funds, by the talented Antonio Chabret. Almadén, still the greatest quicksilver mine in the world, was also known to Solomon and Hiram. It is said that Solomon requisitioned from these mines the cinnabar which was ground into vermilion for decorating his palace at Jerusalem.

An Art Pilgrimage to Europe

The Art Pilgrimage to Europe for artists, teachers, and all who love art and travel, June 19 to September 13, as planned by *Intercollegiate Tours*, under the intellectual guidance of Henry Turner Bailey, Director of the Cleveland School of Art, will offer a rare opportunity to college students who wish to supplement books with first-hand experience, to teachers who wish to increase their acquaintance with the masterpieces, and to the general public, who desire not only the pleasures of travel, but something of its inspirations.

The Archaeological Outlook for Jerusalem

If some of the plans of the present provisional Government of Palestine for the preservation of Jerusalem be carried into execution, that ancient city will be the cynosure of archaeologists. The Jerusalem Government proposes a control over the development of Jerusalem which shall as far as possible leave the antique untouched and provide for the building up of a metropolitan area about the city. Accordingly the plans as proposed would mark out three zones: first, the city within the walls, in which there would be a rigorous control of all new building, along with probably a good deal of condemnation of unworthy buildings. Second, a parked area about the city, which would include many of the sacred sites, and extend as far as Bethany. A large part of this area is actually unoccupied, and it fortunately includes a considerable section of the southern part of the ancient city now lying outside of the walls. This parked circle about the city would be cleaned up and building in general prohibited, so that the city with the old natural environment might agreeably present somewhat of its ancient aspect. The third zone would be devoted to the metropolitan area of the new Jerusalem, and would be the field of all that is best in the art of city-planning. The parked areas could of course be made the object of excavations, and fortunately a large portion of the ancient city could thus be excavated. Under proper governmental control and with the assistance of the learning and wealth of those interested in archaeology, a brilliant future may be expected for the archaeological study of the city which vies with Athens and Rome in the interest of the world.

Our American School by its forwardness in immediately entering upon its work at the conclusion of the war is in a privileged position to do its share in this archaeological future. Before the end of the past year the full staff of the School was on the ground, Director Worrell, Professors Clay and Peters, and the Thayer Fellow of the Institute, Dr. Albright.

ART AND ARCHAEOLOGY

The Summer School of the Pennsylvania Academy

The Pennsylvania Academy of Fine Arts is conducting a summer school at Chester Springs, Chester County, Pa. This will be the fourth year the school has been open and the success of the three former years has been remarkable. During the summer of the school's third year, which began in April, 1919, there was a total enrollment of 169 students, who came not only from Pennsylvania, but from far distant points. The chief object of the Academy in establishing a school in the country is to afford fine art instruction in the open air, with all the beautiful surroundings of nature herself, in order to supplement instruction within the walls of classrooms, and afford an opportunity for the study of art in the summer to school teachers and others who cannot spare the time to study in the winter. The methods of instruction at the Chester Springs school are substantially the same as those at the Academy in Philadelphia during its regular winter courses, special attention, however, being paid to landscape drawing and painting and to the study of sunlight and shade.

American Excavations in Asia Minor

It is nearly forty years since the first work of archaeological investigation in Asia Minor under American auspices was undertaken. From 1881 to 1883 an expedition sent out by the Archaeological Institute of America and directed by J. T. Clarke excavated on the site of ancient Assos in the Troad. The remains of the Doric temple of Athena were entirely unearthed and excavations were extended into various parts of the ancient town with gratifying archaeological results.

In 1909 permission was granted by the Turkish Government to Professor Howard Crosby Butler of Princeton University, editor of this Asia Minor number of ART AND ARCHAEOLOGY, to excavate at Sardis, the capital city of ancient Lydia. Funds for successive campaigns of excavation were furnished by a small group of financiers interested in archaeology and art. At the end of the fourth season a society was formed under the name of "The American Society for the Excavation of Sardis", which proposed to carry on the work of excavation and publish the results.

Work was begun early in the spring of 1910, and was continued in campaigns of six months each year until the end of June, 1914, when the war put an end to the undertaking. It is expected that the work will be resumed as soon as Asia Minor is again tranquilized. The results are briefly described in this number. The rich fund of inscriptions have been published by David M. Robinson in the AMERICAN JOURNAL OF ARCHAEOLOGY.

Since about 1910, Dr. T. Leslie Shear of Columbia University, has been conducting investigations and private excavations on a more modest scale, but with gratifying results, in southwestern Asia Minor and on the Island of Rhodes. More in the line of general exploration, with a view to making a complete survey of Asia Minor, was the work of the late Professor Sterrett of the Cornell University expedition. This expedition reported a large number of sites of archaeological interest and collected a number of inscriptions. The untimely death of Professor Sterrett arrested the execution of his extensive plans for a full report on the ancient sites of Asia Minor.

BOOK CRITIQUES

THE ART BULLETIN. *An Illustrated Quarterly published by the College Art Association of America. Vol. II. Nos. 1 and 2 (September and December, 1919).*

We welcome the appearance of the first two numbers of "The Art Bulletin," the new name under which the College Art Association of America publishes its Bulletin as an illustrated quarterly periodical, with David M. Robinson as Editor-in-chief and John Shapley as Associate Editor. The four annual bulletins heretofore published are taken as Volume I. Vol. II. No. 1 has articles on The Future of the College Art Association, by John Pickard; the Sources of Romanesque Sculpture, by Charles R. Morey; the Significance of Oriental Art, by Ananda Coomaraswamy; Camouflage and Art by Homer Saint Gaudens. No. 2 presents papers on Supply and Demand, by Ellsworth Woodward; A Student of Ancient Ceramics, Antonio Pollajuolo, by Fern Rusk Shapley; Antique Glass, by Gustavus A. Eisen; Recent Contributions to Art History, by John Shapley. Several of these articles are illustrated. All give evidence of the ripe scholarship and abundant output of the members of the Association. We bespeak for THE ART BULLETIN a growing influence in extending the influence and power of the College Art Association, which has recently held its ninth annual meeting at the Cleveland Museum of Art.

M. C.

Parks, their Design, Equipment, and Use, by George Burnap, with frontispiece in color, 163 illustrations and 4 diagrams. Large 8vo. J. B. Lippincott Co., Philadelphia.

George Burnap, the landscape architect of public buildings and grounds, Washington, D. C. has furnished in this handsome volume not only an authoritative manual for park officials, but also a readable volume for every public spirited person interested in city-planning. Mr. Burnap has been for nearly ten years the architect of outdoor Washington and his artistic judgment and good taste are seen in the greater charm of the parks and drive-ways and circles of the Capital City. This is the first book of large scope to be published on the subject, and the author has not only elaborated in his text his theories of park design, but has illustrated from his own photographs almost every recommendation he has made. He treats the relation of park design to city planning, the principles of park design, the use of architecture and sculpture, the decorative use of water, the planting design and disposition of flowers, and many other themes of paramount interest in park embellishment. A book so rich in valuable suggestions and so replete with illustrations of the best that has been accomplished in the parks and public areas of England, France, Italy, Austria, Germany, and North and South America, will prove of service to novice and expert alike in the ideas it unfolds.

M. C.

The Foundations of Classic Architecture, by Herbert Langford Warren. The Macmillan Co., New York, 1919.

In this posthumous work, the late Dean of the Faculty of Architecture of Harvard University has "presented in enduring form the essence of his vital teaching of the history and principles of architecture." The manuscript left at the author's death, ended with the opening words of the final portion, "The Parthenon," and was edited by one of his students, Fiske Kimball, who also completed the volume with the aid of the author's own notes and of notes on his class lectures. The task of collecting and preparing the plans and illustrations, 119 in number, fell mainly on the editor. They have been gathered with great care from the best sources and furnish a body of authentic documents unsurpassed in any other general work discussing ancient architecture.

The author traces the development of the style of Egypt, Mesopotamia, Persia, the Aegean, and Greece to their culmination in the architectural masterpieces of the Acropolis. The historical narrative is suggestive in its presentation of the stages of the evolution of architecture, but far more important is the author's analysis of the fundamental principles of architectural expression, and his exposition of universal forms, such as the classic mouldings and the Greek orders. The illustrations constantly assist the reader in a clear understanding of the subject, and command the warmest praise. This is a work which will be read with profit and interest by students, laymen and architects, and will furnish the basis of knowledge essential for the appreciation of the whole subsequent develop ment of architecture.

M. C.

ART AND ARCHAEOLOGY

American Painters of Yesterday and Today, by Frederick Fairchild Sherman. New York, privately printed, pp. 64.

Mr. Sherman's earlier volume, to which attention was directed in the March issue of ART AND ARCHAEOLOGY, has been followed by another of the same type, both in its dress and in its content.

The format adopted is marked by an individuality under the control of good taste, a combination of qualities in book-making which deserves comment because of its comparative rarity. A binding of the blue boards whose charm Mr. Mosher was perhaps the first to reveal; type which of itself induces the desire to read; board margins of a paper that is pleasant to the touch; abundant illustrations both novel and of good quality—when such characteristics as these are brought together in any specimen of book-making, they deserve commendation on their own account and apart from the text which they set forth.

As for the matter of Mr. Sherman's essays, it is to be questioned whether Mr. Sherman, in stretching his appreciation to include the early imitative work of Harry Watrous, is not being *too* amiable? And a man who can write

pleasantly of this type of painting can hardly be expected to follow Arthur B. Davies in the latest stages of his quest for beauty. So perhaps even a reviewer may point out the inadequacy of the essay on that painter.

Mr. Sherman's talent for writing about paintings appears at its best in his words about men who have not strayed very far from the beaten paths of painting. He places a true estimate upon that once fabulous personage, Benjamin West; he writes well of Wyatt Eaton and George Fuller; he speaks with understanding of the work of Dwight Tryon. And he does good service in pointing out comparatively unfamiliar aspects of J. Francis Murphy and Winslow Homer.

Indeed, the character of all Mr. Sherman's essays is that of brief footnotes to history. He draws passing attention to the lesser-known who who deserve something more than forgetfulness; he throws into momentary relief unfamiliar aspects of the better known. He is the wide-knowledged connoisseur favoring those of more limited range with interesting glimpses through his eyes. The rôle sits well upon him, and a public which has all too little of levelheadedness in art criticism may well hope that he will continue to fulfill that grateful function.

Virgil Barker.

Kindly Mention Art and Archaeology

www.ingramcontent.com/pod-product-compliance
Lightning Source LLC
Chambersburg PA
CBHW081452300326
41935CB00050B/1744